797,885 Books
are available to read at

www.ForgottenBooks.com

Forgotten Books' App
Available for mobile, tablet & eReader

ISBN 978-1-334-45849-1
PIBN 10613244

This book is a reproduction of an important historical work. Forgotten Books uses state-of-the-art technology to digitally reconstruct the work, preserving the original format whilst repairing imperfections present in the aged copy. In rare cases, an imperfection in the original, such as a blemish or missing page, may be replicated in our edition. We do, however, repair the vast majority of imperfections successfully; any imperfections that remain are intentionally left to preserve the state of such historical works.

Forgotten Books is a registered trademark of FB &c Ltd.
Copyright © 2017 FB &c Ltd.
FB &c Ltd, Dalton House, 60 Windsor Avenue, London, SW19 2RR.
Company number 08720141. Registered in England and Wales.

For support please visit www.forgottenbooks.com

1 MONTH OF FREE READING

at
www.ForgottenBooks.com

By purchasing this book you are eligible for one month membership to ForgottenBooks.com, giving you unlimited access to our entire collection of over 700,000 titles via our web site and mobile apps.

To claim your free month visit:
www.forgottenbooks.com/free613244

* Offer is valid for 45 days from date of purchase. Terms and conditions apply.

English
Français
Deutsche
Italiano
Español
Português

www.forgottenbooks.com

Mythology Photography **Fiction**
Fishing Christianity **Art** Cooking
Essays Buddhism Freemasonry
Medicine **Biology** Music **Ancient Egypt** Evolution Carpentry Physics
Dance Geology **Mathematics** Fitness
Shakespeare **Folklore** Yoga Marketing
Confidence Immortality Biographies
Poetry **Psychology** Witchcraft
Electronics Chemistry History **Law**
Accounting **Philosophy** Anthropology
Alchemy Drama Quantum Mechanics
Atheism Sexual Health **Ancient History**
Entrepreneurship Languages Sport
Paleontology Needlework Islam
Metaphysics Investment Archaeology
Parenting Statistics Criminology
Motivational

SOCIALISM
AND
SOCIAL DISCORD.

An Address delivered at the Thirteenth Annual Meeting of the
LIBERTY AND PROPERTY DEFENCE LEAGUE,
FEBRUARY 26TH, 1896.

BY

W. H. MALLOCK.

Published at the Central Offices of the
LIBERTY AND PROPERTY DEFENCE LEAGUE,
7, VICTORIA STREET, LONDON, S.W.

WORKS BY W. H. MALLOCK.

CLASSES AND MASSES; or, Wealth, Wages, and Welfare in the United Kingdom.
A Handbook of Social Facts for Political Thinkers and Speakers. Price 3s. 6d.

Extract from Preface.

"In order to render the information and the arguments conveyed in the following pages as clear and intelligible as possible to the ordinary reader and the ordinary practical man, the statistics and the arguments are alike illustrated by diagrams and pictures. The latter are used as a species of working model, to show the operation of those natural conditions and universal principles of action by which the distribution of wealth and the amount of men's earnings are regulated in every state of society. The former—that is to say, the diagrams as distinguished from the pictures—are used to convey to the eye, at a single glance, the significance of the statistical figures."

LABOUR AND THE POPULAR WELFARE.
Price 1s. paper, and 1s. 6d. cloth.

Opinions of the Press.

"Students who are used to associate economics with a laborious style will be agreeably surprised at the lucidity and simplicity of Mr. Mallock's exposition, the brilliance of his manner, and the aptitude of his illustrations."—*The Times.*

"The book is one of the most valuable contributions that have been offered to the discussion of what has now become *the* problem of social problems.......Regarded as a popularly-written exposure of current economic errors and fallacies, it is without an equal in both comprehensiveness and excellence."—*Liberty Review.*

"In this work Mr. Mallock combats militant Collectivism with every weapon left in the armoury of Individualism.... He outlines with really remarkable lucidity the parts respectively played in production by Land, Fixed Capital (plant), Circulating or Wage Capital, Labour, and Ability."—*Daily Chronicle.*

"'Labour and the Popular Welfare'....is an invitation to the labourer and to the friend of labour to leave off dreaming Socialist dreams that never have been, and never can be, realised, and to study, instead, the forces that are at work in producing national progress and wealth."—*Scotsman.*

"An important and carefully-reasoned treatise. It deserves careful study."—*Daily Telegraph.*

"'Labour and the Popular Welfare' should be studied by the Radicals.....They will find wisdom in it, and much food for reflection."—*The Echo.*

"No one can resist a tribute of admiration to Mr. Mallock for his luminous exposition, and for the exceeding brilliance of his style."—*The Weekly Sun.*

"It may safely be asserted that none can fail to be charmed with the lucidity and logical directness of his work, while its utility as a practical commentary on a recondite, economic, social, and political question cannot be overrated."—*The Spectator.*

"His treatise on the causes of production, the shares in the reward which are due to them respectively, the nature of wealth, and the potentialities of the State in relation to it, is painstaking, persuasive, and brilliant."—*Saturday Review.*

A. & C. BLACK, Soho Square, London.

THE LIBERTY AND PROPERTY DEFENCE LEAGUE.

THIRTEENTH ANNUAL MEETING.

THE Thirteenth Annual Meeting of the Liberty and Property Defence League was held on Wednesday afternoon, February 26th, 1896, in the large hall at Westminster Palace Hotel. Mr. W. H. Mallock presided, and the attendance included :—The Earl of Wemyss, Earl Fortescue, Baron Dimsdale, Viscount Sidmouth, Sir Mountstuart E. Grant Duff, G.C.S.I., Mr. George Palmer (Mercers' Company), Lieut.-Gen. Traill Burroughs, Rev. Richard Wilson, Alderman T. Dundas Pillans, Mr. Harold S. Neale, Mr. A. G. Crowder, J.P., Surgeon Lieut.-Col. Tree, Mr. W. Martin Wood, Mr. J. C. Paget, Mr. Henry Wilson, M.A., Bailie Doig (Glasgow), Mr. William Hillcoat (Glasgow Wine, Spirit, and Beer Trade Association), Mr. James T. Helby, Mr. Thomas Mackay, Mr. G. A. Robinson (Secretary Federated Brewers' Association), Mr. A. Lovell (Secretary North London Property Owners' Association), Mr. L. Cranmer-Byng (Editor of *Senate*), Mrs. Victoria Woodhull-Martin (Editor of *Humanitarian*), Mrs. H. Strickland Constable, Miss Ada Heather-Bigg (Women's Employment Society), Mrs. Frederick Millar, Miss Constance Plumptre, Miss G. King (Society for Promoting the Employment of Women), Councillor Hulton (Salford), Mr. Charles Fairfield, Mr. Alfred Avery (Licensed Victuallers' Defence League of England and Wales), Mr. Augustus Bird, Mr. Ernest James, Mr. H. Jackson Torr, Mr. George Weller, Mr. R. D. de Uphaugh, Mr. Allan J. Hook, Mr. William Carter, Mr. Charles Crouch, Mr. Colby, Mr. Joseph Gething, Mr. James Middlemore, Mr. W. Hartley, Mr. J. T. Bailey and Mr. F.

Walker (Northern Districts Beer and Wine Trade Defence League), Mr. L. D. Hall, Mrs. Yeoman, Miss Mitchell, Mr. R. Oliver, Mr. O. E. Wesslau, Mr. T. Pennington, Mr. A. A. Taylor, Mr. R. N. McDougall, Mr. Neville Tebbutt, and Mr. Frederick Millar (Secretary of the League).

Letters regretting inability to attend were received from Sir Myles Fenton (South-Eastern Railway Company), Mr. J. G. Groves, J.P. (Manchester), and Mr. George Younger (President of the Scottish Licensed Trade Defence Association).

THE EARL OF WEMYSS, Chairman of the Council of the League, said: My Lords, Ladies and Gentlemen,—I beg to move, as Chairman of the Council of the Liberty and Property Defence League, that Mr. W. H. Mallock do take the chair. We are very fortunate in having secured the consent of Mr. W. H. Mallock to preside on this occasion. We know that he is in thorough sympathy with all our efforts. I have not the least notion what he is going to say, but I have no doubt his remarks will be very much to the point, and prove of interest to all who have the good fortune to hear him.

The proposition being agreed to *nem. con.*

Mr. W. H. MALLOCK took the chair and delivered his address, which was as follows:—

Any Society, such as the Liberty and Property Defence League, organised for the performance of practical political work, in accordance with certain general principles, has always before it two tasks, which, though they conduce to the same end, are in themselves different. The one consists of a detailed application of its principles; the other consists of the elucidation and dissemination of its principles. By the detailed application of its principles I mean the organisation of practical opposition, either in Parliament or elsewhere, to any given piece of proposed legislation which, tested by the principles in question, appears directly or indirectly mischievous; and, I believe I may also add to the opposition of mischievous legislation, the promotion of useful legislation, as one of the ways in which this Society practically applies its principles.

Now, with regard to the action of the League in this respect I shall not presume to speak, partly because my knowledge of it is not sufficiently detailed, but principally because it appears to me that an address of the present kind is not the proper vehicle for any discussion of minute details, such as the merits or demerits of this or that particular measure. I imagine myself to be right in saying that the object of these annual addresses—to the number of which I feel honoured by having been asked to contribute—is rather to deal with the general principles which lie behind the particular policy of the League, and which is one of the most valuable functions of the League to disseminate as well as to act upon.

And it seems to me that this dealing with general principles is useful in two ways. In the first place, it is useful by helping us all to realise more fully the nature and the force of the principles which we ourselves hold. In the second place, it may be useful, more particularly to public speakers or to the writers of political literature, by calling attention to certain aspects of economic truth which may, with special advantage, be put before the public at the moment—whether in speech, lecture, debate, newspaper article, or leaflet—aspects which, being at once pertinent and striking, may assist in giving the mass of ordinary men some clearer insight into the nature of those fallacies by which at the moment they are in special danger of being misled.

Sometimes one economic fallacy, or set of fallacies, is most prominent, sometimes another; and agitators and sentimental reformers seem to have an inexhaustible capacity for inventing new ones. I think I shall best repay you for the attention which your presence here promises me by selecting one fallacy which is specially prominent at the present moment, and is, by its mischievous effects on public opinion, doing much to render sound legislation difficult, and, what is still worse, to produce a temper to which sound legislation is unacceptable. It refers to the relation of wages to prices—to the doctrine, as it is called, of the "living wage," and to all the incidents of strikes, class antagonism, and industrial warfare involved in it.

These strikes and antagonisms, as every Socialist admits, are in themselves great evils, and Socialists promulgate their views and recommend their programme on the ground that in a Socialistic State these evils would cease. When all inequalities of classes are abolished, they tell us, class antagonism will be impossible. When there is no employer or capitalist to absorb profits and interest, the mass of the people will enjoy the whole of what they produce. Discontent, therefore, as we now know it, will cease to exist; for when the labourers have all how can they strike for more? We are all familiar with this plausible train of argument, and its mischief is this, that by placing Socialism before the eyes of the wage-earning population as a state of society in which they would be freed from all the evils and drawbacks from which they at present suffer, it tempts them to think that in supporting Socialistic movements, and especially movements directly hostile to employers, they are necessarily doing something to eradicate those causes which from time to time reduce wages which have risen, and certainly prevent them from rising as fast as the wage-earners would wish.

The point to which I am anxious to direct your attention is as follows—that Socialism, even were it realised, would accomplish none of these things, nor even tend to accomplish them. I do not propose to dwell on the arguments and evidence which prove that Socialism is a scheme which never *could* be realised; or is one which, if realised for a time, would produce poverty and misery for all. So far as the point is concerned which I now wish to insist upon, we will waive all these difficulties. We will suppose that all capitalists and private employers have been abolished, that the production of commodities proceeds as successfully as it does now, and that all that portion of the products now taken by the employer is available for distribution amongst the employed. I wish to point out that, even if all this were to happen, industrial disputes would still be as rife as ever, and that discontent and class antagonism, instead of being done away with, would assume only bitterer and more disastrous forms.

In order to understand the case thoroughly, let us begin by considering the catch phrases and arguments which avowed Socialists and sentimental Radicals, or crypto-Socialists, employ, in their speeches and their newspapers, to express and defend their own opinions, for it is these catch phrases and arguments which are the principal means of disseminating fallacies among the working class. They do not express or embody any clear process of thought; but they convey to the mind a conclusion in such a form that it seems to have some foundation of clear thought behind it, and the multitudes of working men who pick them up and employ them are under the impression that in doing so they are clear and advanced thinkers. The most familiar of these phrases and arguments bearing on the present subject are those which cast ridicule on the law of supply and demand as a law which regulates prices, and, through prices, wages. It would, I believe, be impossible to refer to supply and demand before an audience of Radical artizans without exciting among them a derisive laugh, or an exclamation to the effect that "political economy is exploded." It is no doubt true that the more thoughtful of their instructors would not deny that the law of supply and demand had something to do with the settling of prices under the existing system; but they imagine that its existence and operation are arbitrary or accidental, and that under Socialism its operation would be suspended. "There is," they say—and here is their invariable answer—"all the difference in the world between the production of articles for consumption, as they would be produced under Socialism, and the production of articles for purposes of exchange as they are produced now."

Let us start with examining this statement, so constantly repeated, and consider what it means. It means that the community, under the *régime* of Socialism, would *no longer produce for exchange in the way in which it does now;* or, to put the matter conversely, *that the community would produce for consumption in some way radically different from the way in which it does now.* I will first show that this statement, in itself, is so transparently false that it could hardly have imposed on any human being, if it were not that it is used to mask two other propositions, equally false, but at first sight more plausible. Socialism, whatever else it might do or not do, could do nothing to alter the character of production in the above respect; but would leave the producers producing for exchange just as they are doing at the present moment, and producing for consumption in no other sense than the very real sense in which at the present moment they are producing, and necessarily must produce.

We shall understand this more easily by starting with production in its simplest possible form. An isolated individual, such as Robinson Crusoe, will no doubt afford us an example of what Socialists talk about—namely, of production for consumption, as opposed to production for exchange. But the products, in a case like this, will be few and rude in the extreme. This is by no means the state of things which Socialistic reformers contemplate. They contemplate the retention, and, indeed, the multiplication, of all the resources of civilisation ; and there is not a single scientific Socialist who does not understand as fully as Adam Smith did that of all civilisations and all industrial progress the underlying condition is minute division of labour. Now, division of labour, before all things, means this—that of the products needed by the very poorest man in the community, of the very necessaries of life which he cannot live without consuming, he himself shall make only a very small part—perhaps no part at all ; but that he shall make instead something which shall be exchanged for what he consumes. Take, for instance, the case of a sorter at the post-office. He may, accidentally, sort one letter of his own out of a million ; but this is a mere accident. His wages do not come to him in the form of any service which he thus renders to himself, as they would were he a savage building his own hovel. Or, again, take one of the girls who roll cigarettes in the tobacco factories in France. She, very likely, does not smoke at all, and, at all events, no appreciable part of her livelihood comes to her in the form of cigarettes which she herself rolls. And these examples are all the more to the point in that they are taken from industries which Socialists always put forward as examples and instalments of Socialism.

The statement, then, of the Socialists, that production under Socialism will be production for exchange any less than it is now, is a statement which will not stand a single minute's examination. We shall find, however, that it is used to convey two other meanings which, though really equally false, and, moreover, mutually exclusive, are not at first sight by any means so palpably absurd. We shall find that it is used to insinuate either that the true exchange value of the products of each producer will be estimated, under Socialism, according to a new and truer standard, so that whatever commodities a man produces he shall receive a full equivalent for them, which, it is assumed, he does not receive now; or else that the products which the producer receives for his own consumption shall bear no necessary proportion at all to the commodities which he produces; but shall be apportioned to him—as the Socialists say—"not according to his deeds, but according to his needs," or, as the ordinary agitator of to-day says, "according to some standard of decent living." We will consider these two theories in order.

The first theory—namely, that according to which the position of the wage-earner will be bettered by Socialism, because Socialism will secure for him the full exchange value of what he produces—is the theory of Karl Marx. The great doctrine taught by Marx—the doctrine which first gave Socialism a form at once popular and quasi-scientific—was the doctrine that the exchange value of all commodities actually is, and always must be, determined by the amount of ordinary labour embodied in them. Thus, if ten men produce a thousand loaves in a working day of eight hours, and another ten men produce ten pair of boots in the same time, and the price of ten pair of boots is £5, the price of a thousand loaves will be £5 also. And the same will hold good of all other commodities. Let us take as many cigars, as many neckties, as many glasses of beer, as many chromo-lithographs as are made by any ten men working for eight hours, and the price of each aggregate of cigars, neckties, glasses of beer, and chromo-lithographs will be neither more nor less than £5 also. That is to say, the price of everything is merely a multiple of the number of labour-hours embodied in it. Some men, no doubt, Marx admits, may be exceptionally agile and diligent, others exceptionally idle; but, in spite of this, there is an average standard of efficiency which makes an hour of the labour of any one man in any industry practically equal to an hour of the labour of any other man in any other industry. This doctrine is embodied in the well-known Socialist proposal, that metallic money should be superseded by what Socialists call "Labour certificates," which would mean that the possessor of them had expended so many hours of labour in producing some one kind of commodity, and was, therefore, entitled to any other commodity, or set of commodities, which embodied average labour of the same amount.

Now, in this analysis of value there is nothing, if it be taken in by itself, which, according to the Socialists, has any tendency to be revolutionary. It is simply, according to them, an analysis of things as they are at this moment, and always will be. The doctrine becomes revolutionary only when taken in connection with another, which is this: Each group of producers—that is to say, each firm—includes at the present day, along with the producers, a small minority of individuals, who practically rob the others. These men are the employers and capitalists; and, according to the Socialists, the essence of their position is this, that they are the monopolists of the means of production—raw materials, land, workshops, machinery, and so forth; and the others, the great majority, the true producers, the average labourers who alone create value, are unable to exercise their labour or produce anything at all, except with the permission of this small possessing minority, which sells its permissions at the highest price possible—that is to say, by exacting from the majority all the values produced by them, except such as are sufficient to exchange for the barest necessaries of existence. Thus, if we keep to the supposition made just now, and conceive all the firms in the country to consist of ten producers, and assume the value of the commodities produced daily by each group to be £5, and the bare necessaries of life for each man to be purchaseable for three shillings, a capitalist, according to Marx, will take from each of such groups of ten all of the £5 produced by them with the exception of thirty shillings. That is to say, he will take seventy shillings from them, or seven shillings from each man, as his price for allowing them the privilege of working in his yard or factory; and the sole object proposed by Marxian Socialism, so far as any increase in the remuneration of the labourers is concerned, is the expropriation of the capitalist, together with the abolition of this toll of seven shillings imposed by him, and the handing over of the seven shillings to the labourer. In other words, all industrial distress and discontent at the present day is caused, according to Marx, by the appropriation by the employers of the larger portion of the values produced by the hands employed by him; and all that the hands require to render them rich, happy, and contented is the possession of this withheld portion of the values which they alone produce. Once let them get that, and the wage question will automatically settle itself. All the labourers will be remunerated fully, regularly, and equally, whether they work in groups of several thousands constructing an ocean steamship, or in groups of tens or hundreds producing boots, bread, or trousers.

Now, I am not going to dwell here on the purely childish idea, which lies at the bottom of all the reasoning of Karl Marx—the idea that the great employers of this century, the great captains and pioneers of industry, are simply so many beadles sitting at a kind of turnstile, through which the common labourer, the true architect of civilisation, passes into their factories, and, as he passes, extracts a daily toll from him. Ludicrous as this idea is, let us suppose it to be true. Let us suppose that the workers employed by every employer in this kingdom were given free access to all the means of production, and were also able to go on producing. I wish to point out that, even granting the Socialistic State to be an actual working possibility, industrial peace would be as far off as ever.

In order to understand this, let us picture to ourselves—as we easily can do—a state of society with regard to which the ideas of Socialists would be true. Let us suppose a community of three savages, who require only three necessary commodities—bread, clothes, and fuel. Let us suppose one of these makes all the bread, another all the clothes, while the third produces all the fuel; and that, all three of them working an equal number of hours, the first can just make enough bread for three, the second enough clothing for three, and the third can collect just enough fuel for three. It is evident that each of these men will demand, and will necessarily receive, the produce of a third part of the labour hours of the two others, and give the produce of a third part of his own labour hours in exchange. Here, no doubt, we shall have the precise industrial peace which the Socialists promise us. Goods will, perforce, exchange exactly as Marx says they do. They will exchange in proportion to the number of labour hours embodied in them. But this is true in very rude societies only, where the requirements of men are limited to the barest necessaries. Of civilised societies it is not true at all; and it becomes untrue in precise proportion as societies advance towards civilisation and raise themselves above savagery. The error of Marx and of all his followers, in this respect, consists in their failure to realise the profound and essential differences between a rude society, whose products are so few and so necessary that the demand for each is obviously a constant quantity, and the complicated civilisation of to-day, which Marx specially set himself to analyse. The vital difference, so far as demand is concerned, between an advancing civilisation such as our own and a very rude and primitive society depends on the fact that whereas, in the rude society, all production is production of a few commodities which are necessary, and the demand for which is constant, these commodities are, in a civilised state, produced by fewer and ever fewer numbers of men; and the productive powers that are released from the production of necessaries are devoted to the production of superfluities. Thus the problem of value in a civilised society is principally a question of the exchange value of superfluities.

Now the main difference between the demand for bare necessaries and the demand for superfluities is that, while the first is practically fixed, the second is elastic and variable. Let us take instances. A certain amount of bread, or some equivalent food, is a daily necessary for every human being. Tobacco, wine, and theatrical entertainments are superfluities. Some men drink wine, and neither smoke nor care for the play; others do both of these last things, but drink no wine at all; and the practices of men with regard to each, and, consequently, their expenditure or their economic demand varies at different times in their lives. Let us illustrate this fact by going again to our savage community of three persons. Let us imagine that, by some improvement in the arts, all the necessaries which it originally required the labour of all three to make are now produced by one; and that he is able to make necessaries for a fourth man also, which fourth man we will suppose to be added to the community. Here, then, we have one man producing all the necessaries, and the other three available for the production of superfluities. We will suppose that one of these produces wine, another cigars, while the new comer amuses the rest by performances of Punch and Judy. So long as the three original citizens are amused by the performances of their new comrade they may be willing each to give him a fourth part of what they produce—say, a loaf of bread, a bottle of Burgundy, and three cigars daily. But let us suppose that the three grow somewhat tired of his performances, and, though still willing to give him the necessaries of life in return for his efforts, determine that, for three days in the week, they will drink this bottle of Burgundy and smoke these cigars themselves. The utmost the performer could do would be to refuse to perform, unless he received for his performances the superfluities as well as the necessaries. And for three days each week the others would answer him: "Well, in that case, we don't want your performance at all; so, if you refuse to perform on the terms we offer you, you will not only get no superfluities, but no necessaries either." The performer, who would presumably think a poor livelihood better than none, would have to accommodate himself to the terms offered by the others. He would have as many necessaries as before, but he would be docked of half his superfluities. In other words, the exchange value of his performances would have fallen, not because they represented less labour, but because for this labour there was less demand.

And now for these four kinds of labour let us substitute an indefinite number, and for individuals performing each let us substitute groups of individuals, such as great firms and their employees; and we shall have before us civilised society as it is. But the essence of the situation, as I have just described it, will be absolutely unchanged. In any civilised society, from the very fact of its being civilised, there will always be a demand for superfluities of some sort, and to an indefinite extent; for superfluities *are* civilisation on its economic side. But the demand for superfluities of any given kind is liable to constant variations. Let us take the case which we were considering just now—namely, that of dramatic entertainments. As a fact, any civilised society may be relied upon to demand plays; but the demand for the individual plays offered to it varies indefinitely alike in intensity and duration, and has no calculable relation—as managers and actors know—to the amount of labour involved in their production. A still more luminous example is that of a book or a newspaper. The labour involved in setting the type will be the same, whether one copy is sold or a whole edition; but the exchange value of the edition will vary according to the demand, since whatever part may be unsold will be so much waste paper.

Now, all this, so far as it relates to the existing system, is, as I said before, acknowledged even by many Socialists; but these theorists imagine that in some unexplained way this operation of demand on values, and, through values, on the remuneration of manual labour, would be changed, if only the dream of Marx were realised, and if all that part of these values which now goes to the employer were given back to the manual labourer by the State. The great point to insist on is, that such a revolution, even could it be accomplished without injury to the industries in question, would not alter the dependence of values on demand, and the fluctuation of wages accruing to demand, in any way whatever. This is the point that I am specially anxious to explain.

Let us suppose that during any given period the community pays for its cigars to the cigar-makers a million pounds annually, and that half of this goes to the employers and the capitalists. Were the dream of Marx realised, the same gross sum would still be paid, only the half which now goes to the employers would be added to the wages of the operatives; that is to say, their wages would be doubled. But now let us suppose that after this result is accomplished opium-smoking comes into fashion, and that the demand for cigars is so weakened that the public will continue to buy the same number only on condition that they are sold at a reduced price. The million pounds formerly expended will necessarily shrink. Let us say, for example's sake, that it will shrink to seven hundred and fifty thousand pounds. That is to say, the wages of the operatives will be reduced by 25 per cent. So long as one employer takes any portion of the gross value, any reduction in this value may perhaps fall only upon him, and, instead of wages being reduced by 25 per cent., the profits of the employer may be reduced by 50. Thus the workmen are blinded to the real nature of the situation. So far as they are concerned, the employer acts as a buffer. But if once the Socialists could take the employer's profits and make them over to the workmen, the workmen would feel instantly, and with unmitigated severity, every decline in the demand for whatever commodity they might be producing. Let us for a moment apply this reasoning to the case of coal. Suppose the dreams of the men who call themselves "labour leaders" were accomplished, that all mining royalties were abolished, and no interest paid on the capital sunk in collieries, and that the colliers themselves took every penny of the price paid for the coal at the pit's mouth. In that case, if the demand for coal fell, the price of coal at the pit's mouth would fall also, for the fall in demand would simply mean that the great mass of the community would sooner be without a large portion of the coal it now consumes than continue to give the price asked for it. Of about 150,000,000 tons which are consumed in this country annually, about half are consumed, directly or indirectly, on account of superfluities—either indirectly in the manufacture of them, or directly in superfluous fires in private houses; and, even if the colliers succeeded in exacting a higher price for such coal as was necessary, the fact that they could dispose only of a diminished amount for superfluities would inevitably reduce their total receipts, or, in other words, their wages, to the total sum which the public chose to pay. Of course, if the public is determined to have coals at all, it must pay enough to keep the colliers healthy and active; but any minimum limit that rises above this sum is determined not by any fanciful standard of living which the colliers may choose to adopt, but by the price per ton which the consumers as a whole are just willing to pay, and beyond which any advance will so decrease their consumption that the total expenditure in coal will sink faster than the price rises.

This result has nothing to do with the employer or the capitalist. It has little to do with the richer sections of society. Reductions of wages, in such industries as the coal industry at all events, are brought about by the poorer classes, as a whole, rather than the richer; and the more completely we eliminate the figures of the capitalist and the employer from society, the more completely does the imperious bearing of demand on values, on prices, and on wages, show itself.

Let us divide any community into as many groups of

labourers as there are commodities or services demanded by the community at any given time. Let us say there are ten groups, and ten kinds of commodities. Let us start with supposing that the amount of remuneration that goes to each labourer is equal, because the demand for each commodity is in a certain given condition; and then let us take each commodity in succession, and suppose that the desire for it on the part of the producers of the other nine commodities decreases. This means that the producers of the other nine commodities, who have hitherto been giving a tenth part of their products to the producers of the tenth commodity, would prefer either to consume a part—we will say a half—of this tithe themselves rather than give it all, as heretofore, in return for the tenth commodity; and would be willing, if the producers of the tenth commodity would not part with it on these reduced terms, to go without it altogether. This would mean that the tenth group of producers would either be unable to exchange their products at all, or would else have to part with them at half their previous price. But, if they resented this reduction, what remedy would be open to them? Could they strike? A leader of strikes in a Socialistic State would, indeed, see strikes with eyes from which scales had fallen. He would see that a strike among such a group of workers as we have supposed would be one-tenth of the labourers striking against nine-tenths. In fact, we have only to follow the invitation of the Socialists so far as to imagine a State in which the labourers receive everything, to realise that any attempt to make wages, instead of demand, regulate prices would, on the part of whatever group of labourers might be concerned in it, be an attack on the interests of every other labourer in the community.

And these considerations bring us to another point which I said I would touch upon. What I have been endeavouring to make clear thus far is that the wages question would not be set at rest, nor class antagonisms diminished, by allowing each group of wage earners to take the whole exchange values of their joint products. But there still remains another Socialist formula to be discussed, the formula which asserts that wages should be "not according to the workman's deeds, but according to his needs." This is the living wage doctrine stated categorically; and after what has been said already it can be disposed of easily. In the first place, if we accept it, we are completely throwing over not only Karl Marx's theory of value, but every theory of value whatsoever. In the second place, if we act in the way which this doctrine suggests to us, we shall be only disguising the antagonism of interests necessarily resulting from the fluctuation of value, but in no way removing it or diminishing it. If any group of workers finds that the exchange value of its products is not sufficient for its needs; if it finds, in other words, that the rest of the community will not give it for its products as much as it desires and thinks it ought to get, the Socialistic State could alter this state of affairs only by extorting, through taxation, from the rest of the community, a sum sufficient to satisfy the discontented group of workers, and, handing it over to them to supplement the deficiency caused by the diminished prices which their products command. The State, in fact, would stand at the door of the shop in which the discontented workers sold their products; and if the customers would only pay sixpence over the counter for goods which the producers thought should command a shilling, the State would take sixpence from each emerging customer, and obligingly hand it over to the discontented worker inside. The State would thus be forcibly mulcting the larger part of its citizens in order to benefit men who gave them no adequate equivalent. The only difference between this case and the former would be that the hostility of the majority of the citizens would have for its immediate object, not the discontented group of workers, but the State; and, as the State under Socialism would theoretically respond to the will of the majority, it is evident that very soon the claims of the discontented group of workers would be disallowed, and the wages of these workers would be adjusted, not to the value which they set upon themselves, but on the value which the majority of the community set upon the goods they offered to them.

Thus, whatever theory of value we adopt, and whatever attempts we make to regulate the rates of wages which shall be paid to various workers, we see that ultimately the same truth emerges—namely, that the wages of any one group of workers are regulated not by their own desires, but by the desires of all the other workers; and that the employing class, so far as they affect this antagonism at all, modify it, and bear the brunt of it, but have no share in causing it.

And now, throughout the whole continent of Europe, wherever labourers are to any great extent the direct owners of the soil, we see this great fundamental truth coming to the surface, and teaching it to us by an enormous object-lesson. We see the peasant proprietors on one side in favour of the protection of agriculture, and the artizan class of the towns in favour of agricultural free trade. The object of the peasant is to sell the townsman bread as dear as possible, and the object of the townsman is to buy it as cheaply as possible. There is no question of any employer here. It is simply one class of worker against another class of worker.

In all this which I have said I am aware that there is nothing new. But I think that we, in this room, may all flatter ourselves that what we are in search of is not what is new, but what is true; and I think that one of the best uses to which a speaker can put an occasion like the present is by calling attention to some truth which it is specially desirable to emphasise and popularise at the moment, because at the moment masses of men are being deluded into forgetting it. It seems to me that the Liberty and Property Defence League could select no truth which it is more desirable to make plain on platforms, in lectures, in debates, in newspapers or leaflets, than this truth on which I have, I fear, at too great length been insisting—namely, that wages disputes are not, except in a very incidental way, disputes between employed and employer, between workmen and capitalists, but between one group of workmen and, practically, all the rest of the world; and that any attempt to solve such questions by legislation hostile to capital, or by any interference with the free play of economic forces, will not be really to suspend or modify the action of those forces, but merely in the long run to make confusion worse confounded, and to render difficult, if not impossible, those compromises by which alone the frictions of life can be lessened.

THE CHAIRMAN: I now call upon Lord Wemyss to present the Annual Report of the Council.

Lord Wemyss: My Lords, Ladies and Gentlemen,—A vote of thanks to Mr. Mallock for his address will be subsequently duly moved by a gentleman present; and, therefore, all I feel justified in doing now is personally to thank Mr. Mallock for the excellent address he has given us, which, I think, is a most useful, as it is a very unsparing, dissection of the follies and fallacies of the Socialist doctrines of the so-called "labour leaders," who pretend to lead the labouring classes, and who would fain lead them into some Utopia evolved out of their own inner consciousness. Mr. Mallock pointed out that one of their fallacies was the ridicule they sought to cast upon political economy, affecting to treat the principles of Adam Smith as obsolete, as dead and buried, or, in their choice phraseology, as "up a tree." Their disbelief in political economy is just as senseless as if they affected a disbelief in the law of gravitation. Political economy is simply the law of gravitation applied to social matters. I will give you an instance which came under my own notice of the way in which even the most intelligent of "labour leaders" ignore the principles of political economy. Some twenty-five or thirty years ago the late Mr. Macdonald, who was member of Parliament for Stafford, came to me with a petition to Parliament praying for some restrictions to be imposed, with a view of preventing or minimising accidents in collieries. I was then member for Haddington, where there are some coal mines. Mr. Macdonald, I may tell you, began life as a pit boy, and by frugality, perseverance, and self-culture raised himself in the social scale. With the money he saved by working hard in coal-pits in Scotland during the summer he was enabled to attend the classes of Glasgow University in the winter. I remember introducing him to the then Lord Derby, to whom he desired to present a petition; and Lord Derby said: "I am proud to make Mr. Macdonald's acquaintance." Mr. Macdonald did a great many things in the interest of working men, and some of his schemes we succeeded in carrying in Parliament. Ultimately he became member for Stafford. One day he said to me: "When, as a boy, I used to work in coal-pits, the men were then practically slaves, and were sold with pits; but we have got rid of that slavery. Then employers and employed used to be on a very different footing before the law. Under the law of master and servant, if the former broke their contract, the matter was simply the ground of a civil action ; but if the workman committed a breach of contract, the breach was a criminal offence, and he was liable to be seized and brought before a magistrate and punished at once. Well, we have got rid of that. Then Trade Unions were regarded by law as illegal combinations. We have abolished that. And now," he finally remarked, " we mean to make war on the law of supply and demand." (Laughter.) That is an illustration of how the irresistible laws of political economy were regarded by one of the most intelligent representatives of the working classes—a man who raised himself from the humble position of a pit boy to that of member of Parliament for an important constituency. Well, I think Mr. Mallock's address is very valuable, and I only hope that some of the so called "labour leaders" may read it. What I have to do is to put before you the report of the Council of this League for the past year. You have, no doubt, read it. I think it is a very full and very able report. It shows at length the progress that our League has made, it describes how we work, and the good work which has been done. I should like to say that all my part in connection with this report consists in my having perused it nad revised it. It is really due to the energy and ability of Mr. Frederick Millar, who, since the lamented death of Mr. W. C. Crofts, has been the Acting Secretary of the League. Yesterday, I am glad to be able to tell you, the Council of the League, appreciating the energetic and able manner in which Mr. Millar has acted as Secretary since the death of Mr. Crofts, appointed him as the permanent successor of our late-lamented Secretary. (Applause.) The Council at their meeting yesterday were desirous that a misunderstanding which prevails in some quarters with respect to the aims and objects of this League should be, as far as possible, removed. There seems to be some misunderstanding as to the real purposes of this organisation and its *modus operandi*. We have, as you know, nearly 200 different defence societies and corporate bodies, representing important commercial interests and industries, federated with us ; but there are many associations in the country, for whom we do a great deal of work, who hold aloof under the mistaken impression that we are a rival organisation. So far from that being the case, our only desire is the federation of all existing protective associations for one common purpose—that of united resistance in the event of an attack upon any one interest involved in the federation. We wish that, instead of each association working for its own particular interest, and thus subjecting itself to a charge of mere selfishness, we wish for them all to be federated with the League, which has no party politics and knows no party politics, and takes its stand only upon the security of individual liberty and private property. Whenever any interest is attacked or endangered in its liberty or its property, we desire that this League should be the means of focussing, as it were, the power of all these different interests, so that, if any one is attacked, the attack may be resisted by the entire Parliamentary and outside force of all the rest. All for one and one for all, on the broad basis of resistance to undue State or municipal interference with personal liberty and the rights of private enterprise and property, is the principle of the federated action at which this League aims ; and by the federation of all interests with it they can, through it, exercise their united strength of opposition. If that broad aim of our League be made known by those present from different parts of the country to the associations which now hold aloof from us, I trust that before long, instead of being allied with only 200 defence associations, we shall have all such societies federated with the League, numbering in all about 400. (Applause.) To this end I have written a circular letter to all the many other societies as yet unconnected with the League, pointing these facts out to them, and urging them to join us, not in our interest, but in their own, and in the interest of the cause we all represent. In the report of the Council you will find a full account of our doings. There is a good deal said in it about the late General Election. Now, when I say anything in reference to that event pray understand clearly that I do not speak as a party politician. We have no party politics as a League. We stand, as I said just now, in defence of a defined principle. We do not care where a measure comes from if it be good and sound in principle. If it tends to preserve individual liberty and to safeguard the rights of private property, we are bound to support it, as we are bound to oppose any Bill likely to have a contrary effect. We will welcome any measure consonant with our objects, whether it emanates from Socialists, Liberals so-called, Radicals or "crypto-Socialists"—the excellent descriptive name used by Mr. Mallock—Conservatives, or any other party. Having regard to our distinctive principles, the principles this League was formed to uphold and promote, I think we meet this year under very favourable and encouraging circumstances. For there can be no doubt—and I know this is the opinion of those who have to deal with electioneering politics—there can, I say, be no doubt that the late election was in a great measure a revolt against the aims and pernicious tactics of the so-called "labour leaders." (Applause.) Look where the doughty John Burns was at the last election! We all know that he escaped rejection in Battersea only by the skin of his teeth. The election was a revolt, not only on the part of the working, but also of the middle, class, and of all intelligent, independent, and sensible men with a love of liberty and something to lose, against perpetual State and municipal interference with liberty and property—an interference prompted by a desire to catch votes, and to elevate its promoters into positions of emolument and importance. Well, now that the Unionist party have been returned to power with an exceptionally large majority, the question arises: What will they do with it? I have good hope that they will make a good use of their power, or will abstain, at all events, from fussy and meddlesome legislation—legislation likely to interfere with the rights of liberty and property. (Hear, hear.) I will give you my reasons for having good hope that our principles will be safe in the hands of the present Government. There was a deputation the other day to the Home Secretary on the subject of an Eight Hours Bill for miners, and that deputation met with no encouragement from Sir Matthew Ridley, who said that the Government were not prepared to adopt a compulsory Eight Hours Bill. I know the great majority of the Government are opposed to such a measure; but one member of the Ministry—and a very important one—is pledged to eight hours; and there comes the difficulty. There is, however, no chance of an Eight Hours Bill being passed. We had a speech recently from the Prime Minister which fills me with delight. A deputation from the Church of England Temperance Society, headed by the Bishops of London and Durham, had an interview with Lord Salisbury with reference to "temperance" legislation. I am bound to do the Bishops the justice of saying that, if legislation be necessary on this subject, the fact proves that Bishops are, to a great extent, a failure—(laughter)—because it shows they are impotent by moral suasion to induce people to act rightly, and hence desire the strong arm of the law in order to coerce people into doing what they think right. The Bishops' proposals were an admission that their moral influence was unavailing; but my conviction is that the extraordinary improvement which is taking place in the manners and conduct of the people—begotten of better and more widely-diffused education, a keener sense of self-respect, and of the need of self-control—renders such legislation as the Bishops desire wholly unnecessary, even if it were not subversive of the liberty of the community. (Applause.) We now see comparatively few drunken people about. In society, generally, there is a marked and striking improvement in the matter of drinking. To revert to the Bishops. One of the Bishops, I forget which—(cries of "Durham") yes, the Bishop of Durham said, in the course of his remarks to the Premier, that "he thought they were too much inclined to make of the liberty of the subject a kind of idol." What did Lord Salisbury say in reply to this? He said: "I confess to the Bishop of Durham that in many cases I do make an idol of individual liberty, and, dealing only with secular considerations, I consider it the noblest idol before which any human being can bow down." (Applause.) I say those are noble and true words. (Hear, hear.) The head of the Government is, in this respect, a fellow idolater with everybody in this room. Lord Salisbury has a son, Lord Cranborne, a very excellent and able gentleman. I would call your attention to what Lord Cranborne said on the occasion of the second reading of Sir John Lubbock's Early Closing of Shops Bill, on the 19th instant. That Bill practically means this: Given three shops in a street, two of the shopkeepers, by combining, could virtually close the third shop. A majority of the large shopkeepers of London, who are independent of late trading, could, by this measure, shut up all the small shops on the other side of the water, and elsewhere, against the will of the occupiers desirous of conducting their own business in their own way. That, I think, would be a fearful tyranny. (Hear, hear.) The one thing liberty has to dread in these days is the tyranny of majorities. Well, Lord Cranborne pointed out that the principle of Sir John Lubbock's Bill was extremely dangerous and entirely new, inasmuch as it was intended not merely to protect young persons, but to interfere—by diminishing their working hours—with the labour of adults, who had hitherto been deemed able to protect themselves. (Hear, hear.) These are the words of Viscount Cranborne: "He pointed out that the Bill proposed a fundamental change in the principle of English legislation, and he urged that its details should be carefully considered. The principle of the Bill was an entirely new one, because it was intended not merely to protect young persons, but grown men, who had hitherto been considered able to protect themselves. By diminishing the hours of work Parliament might not confer a benefit on the working classes, for shorter hours might mean less pay. As long as they were not overworked, plenty of work was what the working classes required." "Shorter hours might mean less pay." Lord Cranborne might have gone further, and said, "Shorter hours might mean no pay at all," because the restriction might drive trade away from a locality altogether, and transfer capital elsewhere, where the capitalist was not subjected to the tyranny of a two-thirds majority. The *Times*, referring to this Bill, took, I am glad to say, the same view of it. It said: "The object aimed at is, no doubt, an excellent one; but we confess that we regard the Bill with much misgiving. Sir John Lubbock himself confessed that it enables the majority—in this case a two-thirds majority—to compel the minority to act as the majority think reasonable. The principle is a dangerous one, and may take us far. The law, it is true, has often interfered to protect women, children, and young persons; but, if this Bill be carried, it will subject the liberty to work of adult males to the judgment or the wishes of their neighbours. That is hardly consistent with our British idea of individual freedom." Well, I hope that every interest that loves liberty and loves to manage its own affairs will combine to throw out this Bill, which would introduce the thin end of the wedge in the direction of interfering with the liberty of full-grown citizens. Certainly we of this League shall do what we can to cause the rejection of this measure. I maintain that, if a man cannot work as many hours as he likes, if he cannot even get drunk when he likes (if he is fool enough to do so), and if he cannot work for what wages he likes, we are not a free people. (Hear, hear.) That is undeniable. There is one word of comfort more with respect to all this attempted meddlesome, needless, and mischievous legislation. That word fell from the leader of the House of Commons. Mr. Balfour, in a speech which he delivered at Manchester on July 10th last, on the subject of individual liberty, said that "to his mind the very notion that you are to give a majority of the inhabitants of a particular area the right to say what the minority are or are not to do in the matter of their own personal habits, in connection with the mode of life on which the individual alone has the right to pronounce, appears to be utterly revolting to all the principles of individual liberty which he confessed he had thought it was the proud boast of Englishmen to maintain." I have called your attention to these facts to show you that there is danger ahead. You have these two Bills—the Shops Early Closing Bill and the Miners' Eight Hours Bill, and there will probably be many more of a similar kind now that Home Rule is shunted and the course clear for faddists and Socialists to air their pet schemes. Nevertheless, lovers of liberty and freedom like those assembled in this room have cause to be hopeful in regard to the immediate future when they recall the words uttered by Lord Salisbury and Mr. Balfour which I have just quoted. I now lay the report of the Council of the League on the table. (Applause.)

Mr. J. T. HELBY: My Lords, Ladies and Gentlemen,—The resolution which has been placed in my hands runs as follows:—"That the report of the progress and work of the League during the past year, presented by the Council, be adopted." It affords me much pleasure to move this resolution, and, in doing so, very few words are necessary from me, because you have before you the report itself, in which the work of the League is very fully set forth and explained. There are just one or two points which, however, do seem to me to require attention. I have no doubt that the good work which has been done during the past year by the meetings and lectures held under the auspices of this League, and by the literature it has so freely circulated inculcating right principles in the minds of the people, largely prepared the way for that victory at the General Election to which Lord Wemyss has alluded with so much justifiable satisfaction. (Applause.) You, Sir, in your address, referred, I think, specially to the enormous harm which has been done to the trade of this country, diverting a large part of it abroad, owing to the industrial warfare that has been provoked, for their own purposes, by Socialist leaders and agitators. Complaints are sometimes made by the working classes about "sweating"; but, in going about the East-end, I have been struck with the fact that the working classes are themselves primarily responsible for sweating. I have noticed that they are eager to buy boots and clothing at the lowest possible prices—at prices which are only possible on the assumption that those who produced the goods were the victims of the utmost sweating. (Hear, hear.) Therefore, those who most loudly complain of sweating are really the persons who encourage it. With regard to the progress of this League, I can only say that, so long as Lord Wemyss is its head, it cannot fail to progress and prove increasingly useful. With these few words I move the resolution placed in my hands. (Applause.)

Sir Mountstuart Grant-Duff: Mr. Chairman, My Lords Ladies and Gentlemen,—I have very great pleasure in seconding the adoption of the report, which has been circulated, and which is before us. With regard to our Parliamentary activities, I can say nothing, because that is a matter upon which no one can properly speak who is not in Parliament, and who is not in the constant habit of watching what we are doing there, and seeing how we avail ourselves of the times and seasons for maintaining and promoting our principles. Parliament is a place full of currents and counter-currents, and it requires a very wise and watchful man to know when we should resist and when we should yield, when we should go to a certain extent with the stream and when we should not do so. Of our Parliamentary activity I accordingly say nothing; but you, ladies and gentlemen, I am sure, who have followed the work of this Society, will approve of what we are doing, will approve of the publications that we are circulating, and will perceive the excellent effect they are producing. I do not think there is anyone present who has not been pleased by the address of the Chairman to which we have just listened. We are very grateful to Mr. Mallock for coming here, and I am quite certain that his address, although it may not have any effect upon those gentlemen who think that Adam Smith and the Ten Commandments and the multiplication table are all equally obsolete—although, I say, it may not have much effect upon the minds of those gentlemen, yet it will, I am certain, have a very great effect upon everyone who comes to read it with an open mind. (Applause.) I am exceedingly pleased with the remarks which have fallen from Mr. Mallock about our business being not to maintain what was new, unless it was true, but to care only for what was new and true, true and new; and in this connection I recall a very wise line of Owen, the epigrammatist, a remarkable man, who ought to be better known :—

"Seu vetus est verum diligo sive novum."

"I love the truth, whether it be old or whether it be new." (Applause.)

The motion was then adopted.

ALDERMAN PILLANS: Mr. Chairman, My Lords, Ladies and Gentlemen,—I have the greatest pleasure in moving the resolution which has been placed in my hands—namely, "That the following retiring members of the Council be re-elected: The Right Hon. the Earl of Wemyss, Sir W. J. Richmond Cotton, the Hon. Baron Dimsdale, H. C. Stephens, Esq., M.P., and Sir Edward Watkin, Bart." I congratulate myself, and I think I may congratulate every one present, upon having had a highly intellectual treat in the speeches with which we have been favoured this afternoon from the platform. I have pleasure in moving this resolution, because the success which has attended the efforts of this League during last year, and during the whole course of its existence, proves to me, without any further demonstration being necessary, that the management of the League is in most excellent hands; and when I look upon the names which are mentioned in my resolution I can say that, as the principles embodied in this League are sound, so those names as the names of champions of these principles are "familiar in our mouths as household words." When I mention Lord Wemyss I mention a nobleman who has done yeoman service in this great cause for the conservation of individual liberty, whether of person or property, which has been the foundation of the greatness of this country, and the maintenance of which can alone perpetuate that greatness. It is the principle upon which the success of one of the great political parties in the State was built up for generations, and it is a principle dereliction from which has brought that great party down to almost irretrievable ruin. As a Liberal myself of the old school, I have much pleasure in congratulating this Association upon including in its ranks men of all political opinions, united in one common object of maintaining personal liberty, the rights of property, and freedom of contract. Speaking as a Liberal, I hold that no Act of Parliament can disestablish the decalogue and the multiplication table; and I believe that, so far from the principles of Adam Smith being dead and his system obsolete, any attempt to contravene the principles laid down by that great man will be as fatal to the national prosperity now as it would have been at any period of our nation's history. I have joined the Liberty and Property Defence League because it takes its stand upon sound principles, and is prepared to oppose any deviation from those principles, no matter from what party proposals averse thereto may emanate. Lord Wemyss, as I have said, has done yeoman service in the cause we all have at heart, and hence his name appropriately heads the list of retiring members of the Council whose re-election I propose. The other names I have upon my list are the names of gentlemen who, if not so well known as Lord Wemyss, have, nevertheless, ably championed our cause; and I think we could not do better than re-elect them. Under their management this League has contributed largely to the stupendous success of our principles at the last General Election. I do not wish at this stage to trespass upon this distinguished audience by any lengthy disquisition on the principles which this League is formed to champion; but I will say, speaking from my own experience at the last election, I believe the pamphlets disseminated and the action generally taken by the League had a material effect in producing the wonderful upheaval of indignation at the pernicious policy of the late Government which resulted in a Unionist majority of 150. I think this League renders a great service in stiffening the backbone of our politicians. (Hear, hear.) One of the most deplorable features of modern political life is the jelly-fish tendency which seems to actuate politicians on both sides of the House of Commons. I believe that, if they had a little more courage of their opinions, and took their stand upon principle—if they were not so ready to emulate the celebrated American who declared, " These are my opinions, gentlemen, and if they don't suit you they can be altered," they would win greater respect, and be more worthy of support. Let them take their stand upon principle, and if, when tried, they are not found wanting, they would, I think, find a great deal more support in this country than they imagine. Speaking from my own small experience, I may say that, in separating myself from my party on the Local Veto Bill as a protest against that insidious proposal to invade the rights of free-born Englishmen, I found a great deal more support than I anticipated when I took that action. I say this League, if it does nothing else than support and stiffen the resolves of politicians prepared to adhere to sound principle, it fully justifies its existence. I think it will continue to do as good a work in the future as it has done in the past, and I have great pleasure in moving that the retiring members of the Council be re-elected; and I sincerely hope their re-election may, as they deserve, be carried unanimously. (Applause.)

Miss ADA HEATHER-BIGG: Mr. Chairman, My Lords, Ladies and Gentlemen,—I feel that I have a special reason to second the re-election of the retiring members of a Council which includes Lord Wemyss, who has done a great deal to assist the cause of working women when the State has attempted unduly to interfere with their freedom of effort to earn their own livelihood in their own way. Lord Wemyss has seen and realised something of the danger to which women workers are constantly exposed by the action of ignorant and well-meaning people on the one hand, and of male trade unionists and Socialists on the other, the latter being desirous of concentrating all work in factories, the control of which they would fain secure. If one woman works at home, and is assisted by another woman to whom she pays wages, she is liable to have that home visited and searched by an inspector. You may say that is a sentimental grievance, but surely it is an outrage on the liberty of the subject that an inspector—a factory inspector—should be privileged to demand admission into one's home, at any hour of the day, and certainly some part of the night, in order to institute an inquisitorial search. I do not think it mends matters much if the factory inspector is a woman. The infringement of liberty is the same. I felt grateful to Lord Salisbury when he said he elevated individual liberty into an idol before which he bowed. Advocates of State intervention make an idol of the State official. I prefer the nobler idol of individual freedom. (Hear, hear.). I enjoy the personal friendship of a great number of women workers engaged in miscellaneous industries, not only in London, but also in different parts of the country; and well I know from experience that these restrictions, so far from lessening their work and improving their condition, render both far harder. They do not always *lose* employment by reason of the restrictions imposed upon them, but they have to acquiesce in worse conditions of employment and in lower wages in order to *retain* work. These restrictions, too, make it less easy for them to pass into the ranks of small employers. I think, if Mr. Mallock's writings were read more by the working classes, they would realise the fallacy of the Socialist theories by which many of them have hitherto been misguided. (Applause.)

The motion was then carried *nem. con.*

BARON DIMSDALE: It devolves upon me to move a vote of thanks to you, Sir (the Chairman), for your admirable address. A clear statement such as you have given us, dealing with political or great social problems, is one of those things which are most requisite if we are to win the battle of liberty and property. We must bear in mind, too, that the work which has to be done cannot be done altogether in this room, cannot be accomplished even by public meetings. It can and should be done by educating the people in right principles, and by acting on the principle that the welfare—the public business—of England is the private concern of every Englishman. I am sure if this address be widely circulated and read, and if other addresses of a similar character can be delivered and made known in different parts of the country, we shall then enlist a much wider sympathy with the objects we have in view than many people imagine. I was struck with a remark that fell from Lord Wemyss—namely, that if good is to be done in this cause it will not be achieved by the agency of one political party, but of all political parties; for I believe all parties are interested in this movement. We shall, I trust, be able to enlist on behalf of this League the sympathies of men of all shades of political opinion who hold dear the great object we have in view: the maintenance of the just liberty of every Englishman and every Englishwoman. I mention women because I think we shall find in them very wise and satisfactory allies. They can tell us better than we know, or can realise, what are their wants. Personally, as an old member of many women's societies which exercise considerable influence, I feel that we cannot win our cause if our workers are confined to one sex only. With the sympathy of both sexes enlisted in the furtherance of our aims and objects, I believe that success will be assured. I think we can all join heartily in according thanks to Mr. Mallock for his able and interesting address. We have been favoured on these occasions with addresses from very eminent men, including M. Léon Say and Lord Bramwell, the latter now, unhappily for us, no more—addresses which have done much to popularise this League and advance its objects. Not the least interesting address to which the members of this League have been privileged to listen is that of Mr. Mallock. We owe much to him for his address, which dealt so ably with the fallacies that tend at present to obstruct the progress of the individualist movement. (Applause.)

Mr. HENRY WILSON: Mr. Chairman, My Lords, Ladies and Gentlemen,—I have much pleasure in seconding the motion, and in availing myself of this opportunity of testifying, as an old student of economics, to the great assistance I have derived from the writings of Mr. Mallock. This is the first time I have had the pleasure of hearing him, and I am glad to have this opportunity of stating my indebtedness to him for his clear and convincing expositions, going deep down to the root of the subject with which he deals. Even if his readers do not agree with his conclusions, any impartial person—be he a friend or opponent—who follows Mr. Mallock cannot fail to obtain a thorough and complete grasp of the theme of which he treats. Especially is he useful in emphasising that which I consider the principa fallacy of Socialism—that is to say, Socialists always deal with primary, and never heed the secondary, effects of what they propose. They see an evil and propose some remedy, which, possibly, may have the effect of removing the appearance, at any rate, of that evil; but they never seem to give a thought to the other and often far greater evils which such conduct produces. Lord Wemyss gave an instance just now of the fallacious reasoning of a very clever and clear-headed man—the late Mr. Macdonald, some time member for Stafford. I had an amusing instance of fallacious reasoning on the part of a Socialist the other day. Mr. Herbert Burrows was among the speakers at a discussion I attended, and, referring to the heroic conduct of two policemen at a recent fire in London, he implied that such bravery under a Socialistic system would not be exceptional, but universal. (Laughter.) My knowledge of human nature tells me that we are all, when taken unawares, often better than ourselves; and you must not suppose that, because a man in such an emergency as a fire rushes in to rescue life, imperilling his own life in the act, he will not be found equal to the humdrum virtues of every-day life when not observed; and, however many heroic policemen there may be, I do not think any one of them, even in a Socialist State, would be found ready to set his own house on fire on the chance of a policeman being handy to rescue him. (Laughter.) If we adopted the favourite idea of securing to every man at fifty a pension, how are we to suppose that the same intense vigour and industry displayed now would be shown then, the same activity and the same self-reliance? (Applause.)

The resolution was adopted *nem. con.*

THE CHAIRMAN: It only remains for me to thank you

for the very kind attention you have given me. I should also like to thank the other speakers for the most interesting speeches to which I myself have had the privilege of listening. Mr. Burrows's argument about the policemen was in every way worthy of a Socialist. I was thinking as I walked to this room almost the same thing. Socialists pick out a few instances of men who behave well, and then say: " See what humanity is." You may just as well argue that, because the Archbishop of Canterbury does not want to pick pockets, there should be no policemen in Mile End Road. I thank you for the kind attention with which you have listened to me, and I am much obliged to Baron Dimsdale and Mr. Wilson for their kind references to myself.

The proceedings then terminated.

Liberty and Property Defence League.

(To uphold the principle of Liberty, and guard the rights of Labour and Property of all kinds against undue interference by the State; and to encourage Self-help *versus* State-help.)

COUNCIL—1895-96.

THE RIGHT HON. THE EARL OF WEMYSS, *Chairman.*

SIR FREDERICK BRAMWELL, Bart., F.R.S.

SIR W. J. R. COTTON.

The Right Hon. Sir MOUNTSTUART E. GRANT DUFF, G.C.S.I.

The Hon. BARON DIMSDALE.

Alderman Sir JOSEPH DIMSDALE.

SIR MYLES FENTON.

The Right Hon. EARL FORTESCUE.

ALFRED HEWLETT, Esq.

SIR WILLIAM LEWIS, Bart.

W. H. MALLOCK, Esq.

GEORGE PALMER, Esq.

The Right Hon. LORD PENZANCE

H. C. STEPHENS, Esq., M.P.

W. CARRUTHERS WAIN, Esq.

Sir EDWARD W. WATKIN, Bart.

WALTER FARQUHAR, Esq., *Hon. Treasurer.*

And Representatives of *192* Federated Corporate Bodies and Defence Societies, *representing the chief industries and interests in the Kingdom.*

Secretary and Parliamentary Agent: FREDERICK MILLAR.

RECENT PUBLICATIONS

On Sale at the Central Offices of

The Liberty and Property Defence League,

7, VICTORIA STREET, WESTMINSTER.

- HOW TO SAVE VOLUNTARY SCHOOLS. By Canon Hayman, D.D. Price 1d.
- THE PRETENSIONS OF SOCIALISM. By Yves Guyot. Price 1d.
- *THE STATE CONTROL OF LABOUR. By Yves Guyot. Price 1d.
- *LAND NATIONALISATION. By The Hon. Louis Francis Heydon. Price 1d.
- NATIONALISATION OF LAND. By Lord Bramwell. Price 1d. (Seventh edition.)
- *THE SOCIALIST SPECTRE. Speech by the Earl of Wemyss. Price 1d.
- FOR FREEDOM. Three Lectures on the Fallacies of State Socialism. By J. McGavin Sloan. Price 6d.
- GOD'S ENGLAND, OR THE DEVIL'S? A Reply to "Merrie England." By George Brooks. Price 1d.
- THE FALLACIES AND FOLLIES OF SOCIALIST-RADICALISM EXPOSED. By H. Strickland Constable. Price 1s.
- THE LAST STEP TO PROHIBITION. By George Candy, Q.C. Price 6d.
- THE TIED-HOUSE SYSTEM: A Defence of Free Contract and a Plea for "Let Be." Price 4d.
- DRINK. By Lord Bramwell. Price 1d. (107th thousand.)
- *THE REMEDY FOR UNEMPLOYMENT. By Arthur J. Martin. Price 1d.

* Published by the League.

Particulars of Membership and full List of Publications on application.

Every Thursday. Price One Penny.

THE

LIBERTY REVIEW:

A Journal of Politics, Economics, Sociology, and Individualism.

EDITED BY FREDERICK MILLAR.

———◆———

THE *Liberty Review* is the only organ of the English Press which is representative of Individualist thought. It uncompromisingly advocates the right of personal freedom, vigorously upholds the principle of private property, and opposes all forms of Socialism and Socialistic legislation.

The *Liberty Review* is an independent organ, which provides a platform for the free discussion of economic, political, and social problems, and offers a medium for the exposure of the abuses and evils of State and Municipal Government.

The *Liberty Review* is published on the Thursday of each week, and is issued at One Penny. A weekly copy sent post free to any part of the World for 6s. 6d. per annum.

THE LIBERTY REVIEW PUBLISHING COMPANY, Limited,
17, Johnson's Court, Fleet Street, London, E.C.

LIBERTY

A Journal of Politics, [...] Indiv[...]

EDITED BY FRED[...]

THE *Liberty Review* is the [...] Press which is representati[...] It uncompromisingly advoc[...] freedom, vigorously upholds [...] perty, and opposes all forms [...] legislation.

The *Liberty Review* is a [...] provides a platform for the free discussion of economic, political, and social problems, and offers a medium for the exposure of the abuses and evils of State and Municipal Government.

The *Liberty Review* is published on the Thursday of each week, and is issued at One Penny. A weekly copy sent post free to any part of the World for 6s. 6d. per annum.

THE LIBERTY REVIEW PUBLISHING COMPANY, LIMITED, 17, Johnson's Court, Fleet Street, London, E.C.

Every Thursday. Price One Penny.

CPSIA information can be obtained
at www.ICGtesting.com
Printed in the USA
LVHW081454211118
597922LV00011B/842/P